Cover photo © Neal Preston/Retna UK

ISBN 0-634-08794-0

7777 W. BLUEMOUND RD. P.O. BOX 13819 MILWAUKEE, WI 53213

In Australia Contact:
Hal Leonard Australia Pty. Ltd.
4 Lentara Court
Cheltenham, Victoria, 3192 Australia
Email: ausadmin@halleonard.com

For all works contained herein:
Unauthorized copying, arranging, adapting, recording or public performance is an infringement of copyright.
Infringers are liable under the law.

Visit Hal Leonard Online at
www.halleonard.com

4	Bohemian Rhapsody
22	Crazy Little Thing Called Love
36	Hammer to Fall
49	Headlong
70	I Want It All
86	I Was Born to Love You
107	Keep Yourself Alive
120	Killer Queen
130	Now I'm Here
146	Seven Seas of Rhye
158	Somebody to Love
175	Stone Cold Crazy
191	Tie Your Mother Down
208	We Are the Champions
220	We Will Rock You
223	Notation Legend

Bohemian Rhapsody

Words and Music by Freddie Mercury

© 1975 (Renewed 2003) B. FELDMAN & CO., LTD., Trading As TRIDENT MUSIC
All Rights Controlled and Administered by GLENWOOD MUSIC CORP.
All Rights Reserved   International Copyright Secured   Used by Permission

Crazy Little Thing Called Love
Words and Music by Freddie Mercury

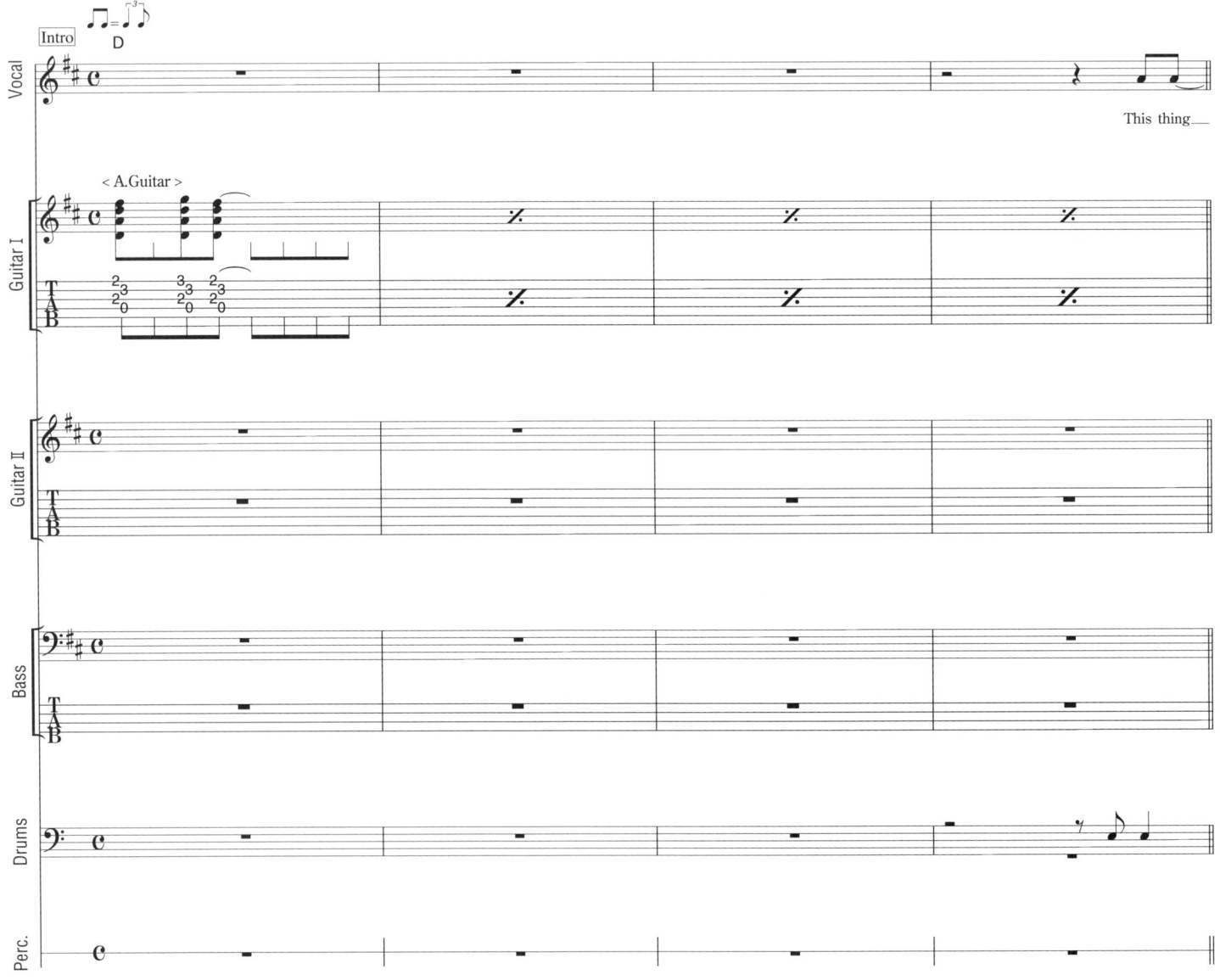

© 1979 QUEEN MUSIC LTD.
All Rights for the U.S. and Canada Controlled and Administered by BEECHWOOD MUSIC CORP.
All Rights for the world excluding the U.S. and Canada Controlled and Administered by EMI MUSIC PUBLISHING LTD.
All Rights Reserved   International Copyright Secured   Used by Permission

Hammer to Fall

Words and Music by Brian May

© 1984 QUEEN MUSIC LTD.
All Rights for the U.S. and Canada Controlled and Administered by BEECHWOOD MUSIC CORP.
All Rights for the world excluding the U.S. and Canada Controlled and Administered by EMI MUSIC PUBLISHING LTD.
All Rights Reserved   International Copyright Secured   Used by Permission

Intro ②
A D(onA) A D(onA) A D(onA) E(onA) A
Vocal
Oh
Other
Guitar I
Guitar II
Bass
Drums
A
A D(onA) A D(onA) A D(onA) E(onA)
Here we stand an' here we fall, his - to - ry won't
ev - 'ry night, an' ev - 'ry day, a lit - tle piece of you is
1x tacet

38

D A E(onA) D(onA) A
Vocal
an - swer the call. Comes to you as to us all. Yeah!
co - ver it all. 'Til one day they call your name.
Other
Guitar I
Guitar II
Bass
Drums
D A A D(onA) A D(onA) A
C
We're just wait - in' for the ham - mer to fall. Yeah!
You know it's time for the ham - mer to fall. Yeah!

40

E F♯m E(onG♯) A D E
Oo, oo, oo, oo, Oh no,
Vocal
Lock your door but rain is pour - ing through your win - dow pane.
Other
Guitar I
Guitar II
Bass
Drums
E E7(onG♯) A E(onD)
Yeah! Ba - by now your strug - gle's all in vain. Yeah,
Vocal
Other
Guitar I
Guitar II
Bass
Drums

E
A
E(onA)
D(onA)
A
Oo.
yeah!
Vocal
Other
Guitar I
Guitar II
Bass
Drums
8va
< E.Guitar 3 >
Vib.
H.C+D
H.C
C.D
P
C
D
Ooh.

43

in the sha-dow of the mush-room cloud. Con-vinced our voic-es can't be heard,

I just wan-na scream it loud-er an' loud-er, an' loud-er. What the hell we fight-ing for? Ah,

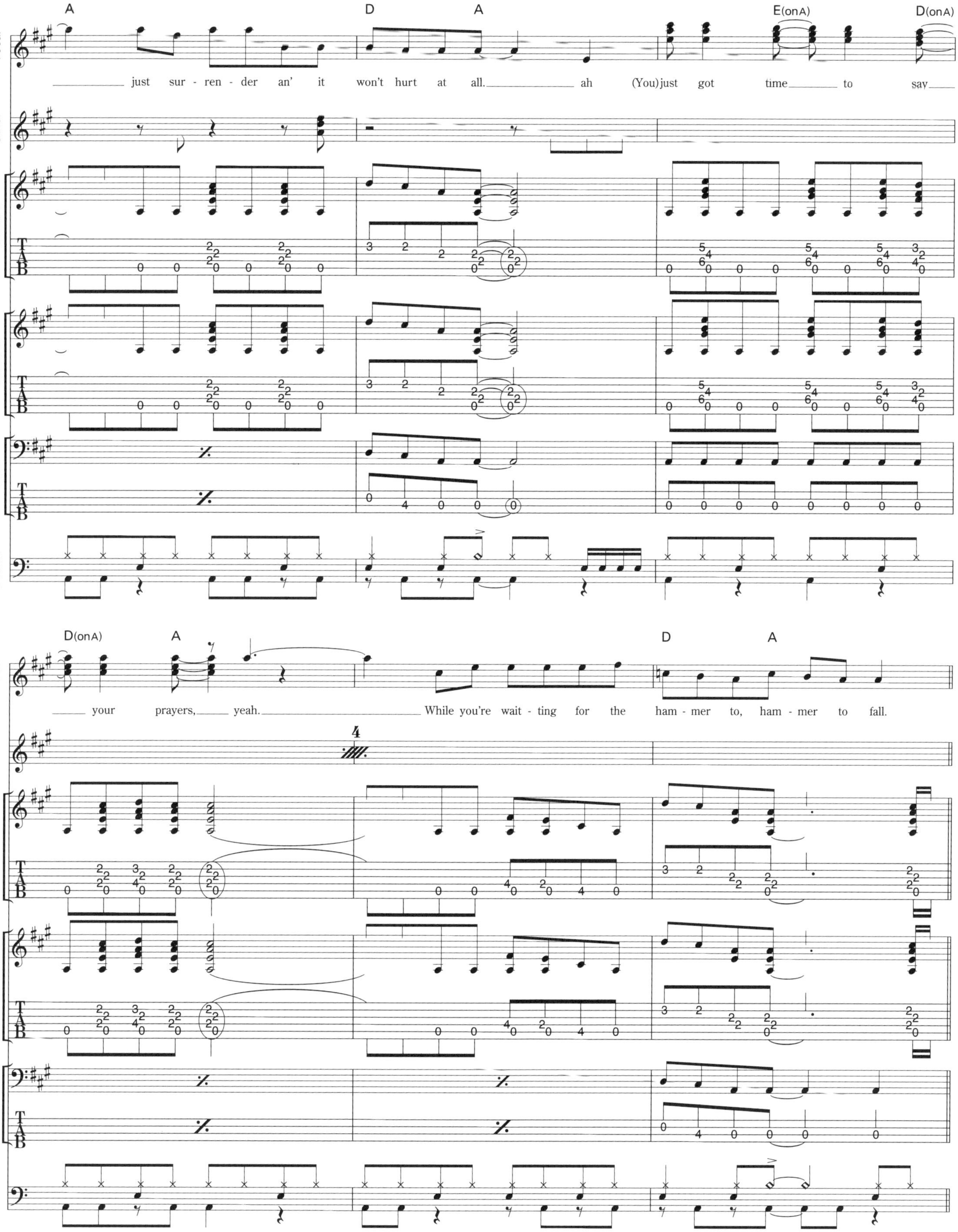
A D A E(onA) D(onA)
Vocal
just sur - ren - der an' it won't hurt at all. ah (You) just got time to say
Other
Guitar I
Guitar II
Bass
Drums
D(onA) A D A
your prayers, yeah. While you're wait - ting for the ham - mer to, ham - mer to fall.
4

H
A
D(onA)
A
D(onA)
E D A
Vocal
Hey!
Yes!
(It's) go - ing to fall, right?
Other
Guitar I
Guitar II
Bass
Drums
A
D(onA)
A
D(onA)
A
D(onA)
E D A
Vocal
Hang on.
You know.
Yeah,
ham - mer to fall.
Other
Guitar I
Guitar II
Bass
Drums

A D(onA) A D(onA) A D(onA) E A
Vocal
Woo!
Ham - mer.
Other
Guitar I
Guitar II
Bass
Drums
A D(onA) A D(onA) A D(onA) E A
Hey,
hey,
woo!

48

Headlong

Words and Music by Freddie Mercury, Brian May, Roger Taylor and John Deacon

© 1991 QUEEN MUSIC LTD.
All Rights for the U.S. and Canada Controlled and Administered by BEECHWOOD MUSIC CORP.
All Rights for the world excluding the U.S. and Canada Controlled and Administered by EMI MUSIC PUBLISHING LTD.
All Rights Reserved   International Copyright Secured   Used by Permission

D
A
D
Vocal
And you're rush - in' head - long, you've got a new goal. And you're rush - in'
Other
Guitar I
Feedback
Feedback
Guitar II
Bass
Drums
D
head - long out of con - trol. And you think you're so strong but there ain't no stop - pin' an' there's

nothin' you can do about it, nothin' you can do, no there's nothin' you can do about it.

No there's nothin' you can, nothin' you can,

nothin' you can do about it. And you're rushin'

head-long you've got a new goal, and you're rushin' head-long out of control. And you think you're

G(onD) D C G
so strong, but there ain't no stop-pin', no there's noth-in' you can do a-bout it. Yeah!
D
Vocal
Other
Guitar I
Guitar II
Bass
Drums

54

G(onB)
D
Oh,
hoop did - dy do. She used to be a wom - an with a hot dog stand.
hoop did - dy do. soon the fire starts a rag - in', gets 'em more than half cra - zy.
Vocal
Other
Guitar I
Guitar II
Bass
Drums
C
G(onB)
D
A
Hoop did - dy did - dy, hoop did - dy do. Now you got soup in the
Hoop did - dy did - dy, hoop did - dy do. (Ooh,) now they start freak - in' ev - 'ry

A
laun - dry bag. Now you got strings, you're gon - na lose your rag. You're
way you turn. You can't stop walk - ing 'cause your feet got burned. It
Vocal
Other
Guitar I
Guitar II
Bass
Drums
A
G
F♯
get - tin' in a fight then it ain't so groov - y when you're scream - in' in the night, "Let me
ain't no time to fig - ure wrong from right, 'cause rea - son's out the win - dow, bet - ter
Vocal
Other
Guitar I
Guitar II
Bass
Drums

1.
A G F D
Vocal
out of this cheap 'B' mo - vie."
Other
Guitar I
Guitar II
Arm.
Arm.
Bass
Drums
E
D
Head - long, down the high - way, and you're rush - in' head - long out of con - trol. And you think you're

D
F
Vocal
so strong but there ain't no stop-pin' and you can't stop rock-in', an' there's noth-in' you can, noth-in' you can,
Other
Guitar I
Guitar II
Bass
Drums
G
D
noth-in' you can do a-bout it.

59

G
D
Vocal
head - long, head - long, Out of con - trol,
yeah, you think you're
Other
Guitar I
S
S
Guitar II
Bass
Drums
D
Vocal
so strong, there ain't no stop - pin' an' there's noth - in' you, noth - in' you, noth - in' you can do a - bout it, at all.
Other
Guitar I
Guitar II
Bass
Drums

61

D
Vocal
Other
Guitar I
H
Guitar II
Bass
Port Down
Port Down
Drums
D
Vocal
Other
Guitar I
Guitar II
Bass
Drums
Syn.Dr.
(Syn.Dr.)

63

64

Al - right, go.

And you're rush - in' head - long down the

66

67

68

D C
Vocal
head - long.
Other
Guitar I
H
Guitar II
8va
Vib.
1H.C
D
C
Bass
Drums
D
Head-long,
F G F G F G
G F G F D
head - long.
< Delay >
(8va)
Arm.

I Want It All

Words and Music by Freddie Mercury, Brian May, Roger Taylor and John Deacon

Lyrics: I want it all, I want it all, I want it all, an' I want it

71

Vocal
Other
Guitar I
Guitar II
Bass
Drums
A G A
Bm A
Bm A Bm
G D(onF♯) G
creep - er, light on his feet. (A) young fight-er scream-ing with no time for doubt, with the pain and
Vib.
C D P
A G A
Bm A
D
D
A
an - ger, can't see a way out. "It ain't much I'm ask - ing" I heard him say. Got-ta find me a
(A.Guitar)
Vib.

A G E Bm A Bm G D(onF♯) G
fu - ture, move out (of) my way. I want it all, I want it all, I want it
Vocal
Other
Guitar I
Guitar II
Bass
Drums
A G A Bm A Bm A Bm G D(onF♯) G
all, an' I want it now. I want it all, I want it all, I want it
4
P
H

74

75

A G H Bm A Bm G D(onF♯) G
Vocal
fu - ture (for) the the dreams of youth. I want it all, I want it all, I want it
Other
Guitar I
Guitar II
Bass
Drums
A G A Bm A Bm A Bm G D(onF♯) G
all, (an') I want it now. I want it all, I want it all, I want it

all, (an') I want it now.

I'm a man with a one track mind, so much to do in one life-time. Not a man for com-pro-mise an'

77

78

79

80

Bm
G
A
Esus4
E
Vocal
Other
Guitar I
Guitar II
Bass
Drums
8va
Vib.
C
D
P

Bm
G
Vocal
Other
Guitar I
Guitar II
Bass
Drums
H.C
C
A
G D(onF♯) G D(onF♯) A(onG)
D
P

A(onG)
Tempo - I
K
D(onF♯)
G
A
G
A
(It) ain't much I'm ask - ing if you want the truth. Here's to the
(8va)
A
G
L
Bm
G
fu - ture, hear the cry of youth. I want it all, I want it all, I want it
Vocal
Other
Guitar I
Guitar II
Bass
Drums

A
Bm
A
Bm
A
Bm
G
D(onF♯)G
Vocal
all,
an' I
want
it
now.
I
want
it
all,
I
want
it
all,
I
want
it
Other
Guitar I
H
Guitar II
Bass
H
Drums
A
G
A
Bm
A
Bm
A
Bm
Vocal
all,
and I
want
it
now.
Other
Guitar I
8va
C
H.C
H.C
Vib.
C
H P
C
Vib.
Guitar II
Bass
Drums

now.
G D(onF♯) G
A G A
Bm A
Vocal
I want it.
Other
4
Guitar I
Guitar II
C
P
Bass
Drums
A G
I want it, I want it.
Woo, Ha!
Fill
8va
C.D
P+H
S

I Was Born to Love You

Words and Music by Freddie Mercury

© 1995 MERCURY SONGS LTD.
Rights Assigned to EMI MUSIC PUBLISHING LTD.
All Rights for the U.S. and Canada Controlled and Administered by BEECHWOOD MUSIC CORP.
All Rights Reserved   International Copyright Secured   Used by Permission

87

B♭m
E♭
A♭
Vocal
ev - 'ry sin - gle day.
Other
8va bassa
< Synth.Bass >
8va
W.C
Guitar I
Guitar II
Bass
(8va)
Drums
A♭
Alright.
Hey, hey.
Arm.
(Arm.)

B
A♭
Cm
D♭
Fm(onC)
D♭
Fm(onC)
Vocal
I was born to love you, with
Other
Guitar I
M
(M)
Guitar II
Bass
Drums
B♭m
E♭
E♭(onD♭)
E♭(onC)
E♭(onB♭)
ev - 'ry sin - gle beat of my heart. Yes,
S

90

C
A♭
Cm
Vocal
one for me. I am the man for you. You were made for me. You're my ec - sta - sy. If I was
Other
Guitar I
Guitar II
Bass
Drums
D♭
B♭m
giv - en ev - 'ry op - por - tu - ni - ty I'd kill for your love. So take a

D
E♭
Cm
Vocal
chance with me, let me ro - mance with you, I'm caught in a dream and my dream's come true. It's so
Other
8va bassa
Guitar I
M
Guitar II
Bass
Drums
Fm
B♭sus4
B♭
hard to be-lieve, this is hap-p'ning to me. An a - maz - ing feel - ing

E♭sus4
E♭
E
A♭
Cm
Vocal
com - in' through. I was born to
Other
(8va bassa)
Guitar I
Guitar II
g.
Bass
Drums
D♭
Fm(onC)
D♭
Fm(onC)
B♭m
love you, with ev - 'ry sin - gle beat of my
(M)
M

heart. Yes, I was born to take care of you, honey, ev-'ry sin-gle day of my

95

D♭
B♭(onD)
A♭
E♭(onG)
Vocal
love you, love you, love you.
Born to love you,
born to love you, yes.
Other
8va bassa
Guitar I
g.
Guitar II
Bass
Drums
Fm
B♭
A♭
(Born) I was born to love you.
Born to love you,
born to love you, ev -
M

E♭
'ry sin - gle day, day, day, day, day, day, of my life.
G
A♭
Cm
D♭
Fm(onC)
Ooh.
Port.D
8va
Vocal
Other
Guitar I
Guitar II
Bass
Drums

98

Fm
B♭
Vocal
Other
Guitar I
Guitar II
Bass
Drums
An a - maz - ing
B♭
E♭
A♭
I
feel - ing, com - in' through.
I was

100

Cm D♭ Fm(onC) D♭ Fm(onC) B♭m
born to take care of you, ev - 'ry sin - gle day
Vocal
Other
Guitar I
Guitar II
Bass
Drums
E♭sus4 E♭ A♭ B♭m
of my life. Yes, I was
J

E♭
A♭
B♭m
Vocal
born to love you, ev - 'ry
Other
Guitar I
Guitar II
Bass
Drums
E♭
A♭
sin - gle day of my life.
8va bassa
Arm.
Arm.

Go, ooh. (I love you babe.)

Yes, born to love. Yes, I was born to love you.

A♭
D♭
E♭
Vocal
Other
Guitar I
Guitar II
Bass
Drums
Hey,
I wan - na love you, love you, love you
E♭
A♭
I wan - na love you,
yeah, yeah.
8va
H.C
D
P
g.
M

105

E♭
A♭
Cm
D♭
Vocal
I want to love you, love you,
Other
Guitar I
Arm.
Arm.
Guitar II
Bass
Drums
Fm(onC) D♭ Fm(onC) B♭m
E♭
love you, yeah, give it to me.
M
F.O.

Keep Yourself Alive

Words and Music by Brian May

【Tuning : Half Step Down】

108

109

110

crossed a mil-li-on riv-ers an' I rode a mil-lion miles, then I'd still be where I start-ed, bread an'
ev-'ry-thing I need, to feed my bod-y an' my soul, an' I'll grow a lit-tle big-ger, may-be

but-ter for a smile. Well, I sold a mil-li-on mir-rors in a shop in Al-ley Way, but I
that can be my goal. I was told a mil-lion times, of all the peo-ple in my way. How I

F♯ B F♯m C♯ D
Vocal
nev-er saw my face in an-y win - dow, an-y day. Well, they say your folks are tel-ling you "Be a su-per-star," but I
had to keep on try-in', an' get bet-ter ev-'ry day. But if I crossed a mil-lion riv-ers and I rode a mil-lion miles then I'd
Guitar I
Guitar II
(M)
Bass
Drums
A B♭ F E♭ A♭
tell you just be sa-tis-fied, and stay right where you are. Keep (1.2.3.) Keep your-self a-live,
still be where I start-ed, same as when I start-ed.
g. C Vib. 2x H S

keep your-self a-live. (1.2.) Take you all your time an' mon-ey, hon-ey, you'll sur-vive.
(3.) Take you all your time an' mon-ey to keep me sa-tis-fied.

114

(3.) Well, I've

116

117

Do you think you're bet-ter ev-'ry day? No, I just think I'm two steps near-er to my grave.

Keep your-self a-live, keep your-self a-live. you

Vocal
Guitar I
Guitar II
Bass
Drums
E♭ G(onD) Cm A♭ B♭ E♭
M
F♯ B
take your time an' take my mon-ey, keep your-self a-live.
Keep your-self a-live,
F♯ C♯ F♯ A♯(onF) D♯m B C♯ F♯
keep your-self a-live.
All you peo - ple keep your-self a-live.
Vib.
8va
H
P
S
H.C
C
D
Repeat & F.O.

Killer Queen

Words and Music by Freddie Mercury

© 1974 (Renewed 2002) B. FELDMAN & CO., LTD., Trading As TRIDENT MUSIC
All Rights Controlled and Administered by GLENWOOD MUSIC CORP.
All Rights Reserved International Copyright Secured Used by Permission

B♭7 Cm7 E♭ E♭maj7(onD) E♭7(onD) A♭
B
just like Ma - rie An - toi - nette. A built in a - re - me - dy for Krus - chev and Ken - ne - dy at
spoke just like a bar - on - ess. Met a man from Chi - na, went down to Gei - sha Mi - nah,
Vocal
Other
Guitar I
Guitar II
Bass
Drums
Vib.
(2x only)
C
g.
Hoo
Chorus 2x only
Hu
Kill - er,
A♭m7 E♭(onB♭) A♭(onB♭) B♭7
an - y - time an in - vi - ta - tion you can't de - cline.
then a - gain in - ci - den - t'ly if you're that way in - clined. Per - fume came
kill - er, she's a kill - er Queen

C
G Cm B♭ E♭ D7 Gm F7
Vocal
Ca - vi - ar and cig - a - rettes, well versed in e - ti - quette, ex - tr'or - di - na - ri - ly nice. She's a
nat - 'ral - ly from Par - is, for cars she couldn't care - less, fas - ti - di - ous and pre - cise. She's a
Other
Guitar I
Guitar II
Nat - u - ral - ly!
(2x only)
Bass
2x
8va
Drums
D
B♭ Dm Gm Dm Gm A7 Dm7
kill - er queen, gun - pow - der, gel - a - tine, dy - na - mite with a la - ser beam.
D.S.2x only
W.H.C
g.

123

F(11) F F(11)
Vocal
To a-
Other
Guitar I
8va
Vib.
C
S
Guitar II
(8va)
Bass
g.
Drums
D.S.①
Coda ①
G
A Dm7 A Dm G Cm G Cm F
U D P

125

B♭7 Cm7 I E♭ E♭maj7(onD) E♭7(onD♭) A♭
Vocal
Other
Guitar I
Guitar II
Bass
Drums
Vib.
< ( )=E.Guitar 3 >
8va
g.
A♭m7 E♭(onB♭) A♭(onB♭) B♭
H.C

Vocal
Other
Guitar I
Guitar II
Bass
Drums
B♭
B♭7
J
G
Cm
B♭
E♭
Drop ___ of a hat she's as will ing as, ___
play - ful as a pus - sy cat. ___ Then mo - ment - a - ri - ly out of action, tem - po - rar - i - ly out of gas, ___ to
Ooh, ___
Ooh, ___
da, ___
Vib.
(8va)
H.C
1H.C
C
U
UD

128

129

Now I'm Here

Words and Music by Brian May

A
D
C
Vocal
look a - round, a-round, a-round, a-round, a-round,
Other
Guitar I
Guitar II
Bass
Drums
B♭
C
D
but you won't see me.
Now I'm here.

132

133

D
E B A D A B F♯
Vocal
Other
Guitar I
Guitar II
Bass
Drums
Wow!
Vib.
E D A
E
B
A ba - by I was when you
Ooh, a thin moon me in a smoke -
< Chorus >
2x only
(2x only)
Yeah
M

135

139

140

141

Down in the cit-y just a-you and me. Ah!

Don't I love_____ you_____ so.

Go, go, ___ go, lit - tle queen - ie.

145

Seven Seas of Rhye

Words and Music by Freddie Mercury

© 1973 (Renewed 2001) B. FELDMAN & CO., LTD., Trading As TRIDENT MUSIC
All Rights for the U.S. and Canada Controlled and Administered by GLENWOOD MUSIC CORP.
All Rights Reserved   International Copyright Secured   Used by Permission

147

C
D
A
G
Vocal
Other
Guitar I
Guitar II
Bass
Drums
Fear me, you lords and la - dy preach - ers. I de - scend up - on your earth from the
hear me, you peers and priv - y coun - cil - ors? I stand be - fore you, nak - ed to the eyes.
skies. I com - mand your ver - y souls, you un - be - liev - ers. Bring be - fore
I will de - stroy a - ny man who dares a - buse my trust. I
2x only
8va
Vib.
< ( )=Another Guitar >
U D
U
D

149

150

G
D(onF♯)
Em7
D
Vocal
-ev - er.
ev - er,
ev - er.
Other
Guitar I
8va
Guitar II
Bass
Drums
D
F
B♭
E♭
B♭
E♭
H
Q.C
C
Vib.
U
UD
P

152

D
G
H
Vocal
Other
Guitar I
Guitar II
Bass
Drums
Storm the mas - ter mar-a - thon; I'll
g.
C
G(onB)
I'll sur - vive, I'll sur-vive, I'll sur -
fly through by flash and thun - der fire and I'll sur - vive.

Am
G(onB)
C
A7(onC♯)
D
-vive, I'll sur-vive, I'll sur-vive, I'll sur-vive, I'll sur-vive.
Vocal
Then I'll de-fy the laws of na-ture and come out a-live.
Other
Guitar I
Guitar II
Bass
Drums
D
I
D
Then I'll get you! Be gone with you, you shod and shad-y sen-a-tors.
Arm.D
Arm.D
6

155

Gm6
D
Vocal
take you to the Sev-en Seas of Rhyc.
Other
Guitar I
Vib.
C
U D
P
H
Guitar II
Bass
g.
Drums

J
D
Vocal
Other
Guitar I
Vib.
P
S
H
Guitar II
UD
Bass
Drums

157

Somebody to Love

Words and Music by Freddie Mercury

© 1976 QUEEN MUSIC LTD.
All Rights for the U.S. and Canada Controlled and Administered by BEECHWOOD MUSIC CORP.
All Rights for the world excluding the U.S. and Canada Controlled and Administered by EMI MUSIC PUBLISHING LTD.
All Rights Reserved   International Copyright Secured   Used by Permission

Vocal
Other
Keyboard
Guitar
Bass
Drums
A♭
A
A♭
E♭(onG)
Em7
D♭
Ooh, ooh,
love?
E♭7
B
A♭
E♭(onG)
Fm7
A♭
B♭7
ooh. Each morn - ing I get up, I die a lit - tle, can bare - ly stand on my
hard ev - 'ry day of my life, I work till I ache my
feel, I got no rhy - thm, I'll just keep los - ing my
1x tacet
(2x) He works hard.
(3x) love.

Vocal
Other
Keyboard
Guitar
Bass
Drums
E♭7
A♭
E♭(onG)
Fm7
B♭7
feet. Take a look in the mir - ror and cry, Lord, what you're do - in' to
bones. At the end, I take home my hard-earned pay all
beat. I'm O.K., I'm al - right, I ain't gon - na face
Take a look at your - self in the mir - ror and cry, yeah,
At the end of the day, His own,
He'll just keep los - ing and los - ing. He's al - right, he's al - right, yeah,
4
E♭7
A♭
B♭7
E♭7
B♭(onD)
to Φ②
me. I have spent all my years in be - liev - ing you, but I just can't get no re -
on my own. I get down on my knees and I start to pray 'til the tears run down from my
no de - feat. I just gotta get out of this pris - on cell, some - day I'm gon - na be
yeah. Ooh, be - liev - ing you, I just can't get no re -
goes home on his own. Down, knees, praise the Lord, ooh. Ooh,
yeah. Ooh, ooh, this pris - on cell, some - day I'm gon - na be

E♭7
A♭
C
E♭(onG)
Vocal
lief, Lord. Some - bod - y, ooh, some - bod - y, can an - y - bod - y
eyes, Lord. Some - bod - y, ooh, some - bod - y, can an - y - bod - y
Ooh, some - bod - y, ooh, can an - y - bod - y
8va
Other
lief, Lord. Some - bod - y, some - bod - y,
ooh, Lord. Some - bod - y, please (1.2.3.) an - y - bod - y
some - bod - y, some - bod - y,
Keyboard
3x
Vib.
Guitar
T A B
Bass
Drums
Fm7
D♭maj9
E♭7
1.
A♭
A♭(onG)
find me some - bod - y to love?
find me some - bod - y to
find me some - bod - y to love?
2x only
find me Can a - ny -

162

Vocal
Other
Keyboard
Guitar
Bass
Drums
D♭
F♯
day, I've tried, I've tried, I've tried, but ev - 'ry bod-y
ev - 'ry day, tried, I've tried, I've tried, ooh,
F♯
F♯dim
wants to put me down. They say I'm go - in' cra - zy.
ooh.

E
B♭7
Vocal
They say I got a lot of wa-ter in my brain. I got no com-mon sense,
Other
ah, he's got
Keyboard
Guitar
Bass
Drums
B♭7
Fm7
E♭7
no - bod-y left to be - lieve. Yeah.
no - bod-y left to be - lieve. Yeah, yeah,
U D U D

165

166

167

A♭
Vocal
Find me, find me, find.
Other
find me some - bod - y to love, find me some - bod - y to love,
Keyboard
Guitar
T
A
B
Bass
4 4 4 4 4 4
Drums
A♭
Vocal
Ooh,
Other
find me some - bod - y to love, find me some - bod - y to love,
Keyboard
Guitar
Bass
Drums

169

A♭
Vocal
Can an - y - bod - y find me
Other
some - bod - y find me some - bod - y to love. an - y - bod - y find me
Keyboard
Guitar
Bass
Drums
D♭
a tempo
some - bod - y to love?

H
A♭
A♭(onG)
Fm7
D♭
E♭7
Vocal
Other
Find me some - bod - y to
Keyboard
Guitar
Bass
Drums
Ooh,
find
love,
find me some - bod - y to

172

A♭
A♭(onG)
Fm7
D♭
E♭7
Vocal
some - bod - y to love.
Ooh,
Other
love.
Find me
some - bod - y
to
Keyboard
Guitar
Bass
Drums
A♭
A♭(onG)
Fm7
D♭
E♭7
Vocal
bod - y, bod - y, bod - y, some - bod - y to
Other
love.
Find me
some - bod - y
to
Keyboard
Guitar
Bass
Drums

A♭
A♭(onG)
Fm7
D♭
E♭7
Vocal
love. An - y - bod - y, an - y - where, an - y - bod - y find me some - bod - y to love. Whoa, whoa, whoa, whoa, whoa,
Other
love. Find me some - bo - dy to
Keyboard
Guitar
Bass
Drums
Free Tempo
A♭
whoa, Find me, find me, find me, find me.
love.
H
g.

Stone Cold Crazy

Words and Music by Freddie Mercury, Brian May, Roger Taylor and John Deacon

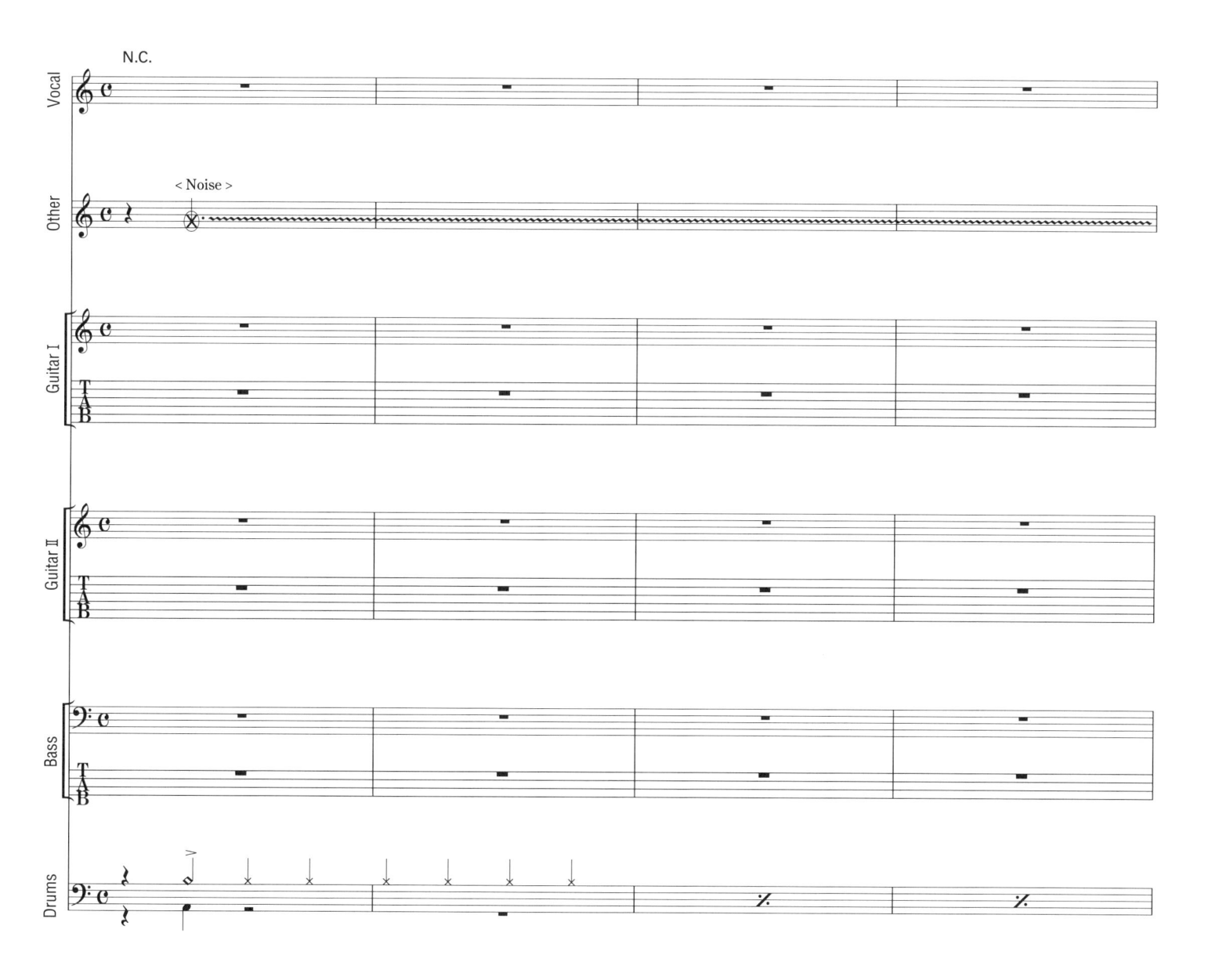

© 1974 (Renewed 2002) B. FELDMAN & CO., LTD. Trading As TRIDENT MUSIC
All Rights Controlled and Administered by GLENWOOD MUSIC CORP.
All Rights Reserved   International Copyright Secured   Used by Permission

Intro
(3 times Repeat)
N.C.
F G F B♭
Vocal
Other
Guitar I
Guitar II
Bass
Drums
F G B♭ C B C C♯ D F G F B♭
H

Sleep-in' ve-ry sound-ly on a Sat-ur-day morn - ing, I was dream-in' I was Al Ca-pone. There's a

178

179

C
F G F B♭ F G B♭ C B C C♯ D
Vocal
Other
Guitar I
Guitar II
Bass
Drums
F G F B♭ F G B♭ C B C C♯ D G A A♯
Woo!
Ah!

181

E
F G F B♭ F G B♭ C B C C♯ D
Vocal
Other
Guitar I
Guitar II
Bass
Drums
F G F B♭ F G B♭ C B C C♯ D
Vocal
Other
Guitar I
Guitar II
Bass
Drums
4
H

F
G
Vocal
Rain - y af - ter - noon I got - ta blow a ty - phoon an' I'm playin' on my slide trom - bone.
Other
Guitar I
Guitar II
Bass
Drums
G
B♭(onG)
An - y - more, an - y - more, can - not take it an - y - more, got - ta get a - way from this stone cold floor.

184

B
Vocal
Other
Guitar I
Guitar II
H
S
Bass
Drums
B
Vocal
Other
Guitar I
Guitar II
C
Delay →
U D
Bass
Drums

186

187

188

gotta get me, get up an' run. They got the si- rens loose, I ran right
out- ta juice. They're gon-na put me in a cell. If I can't go to hea-ven will they

190

Tie Your Mother Down
Words and Music by Brian May

© 1976, 1977 QUEEN MUSIC LTD.
All Rights for the U.S. and Canada Controlled and Administered by BEECHWOOD MUSIC CORP.
All Rights for the world excluding the U.S. and Canada Controlled and Administered by EMI MUSIC PUBLISHING LTD.
All Rights Reserved   International Copyright Secured   Used by Permission

192

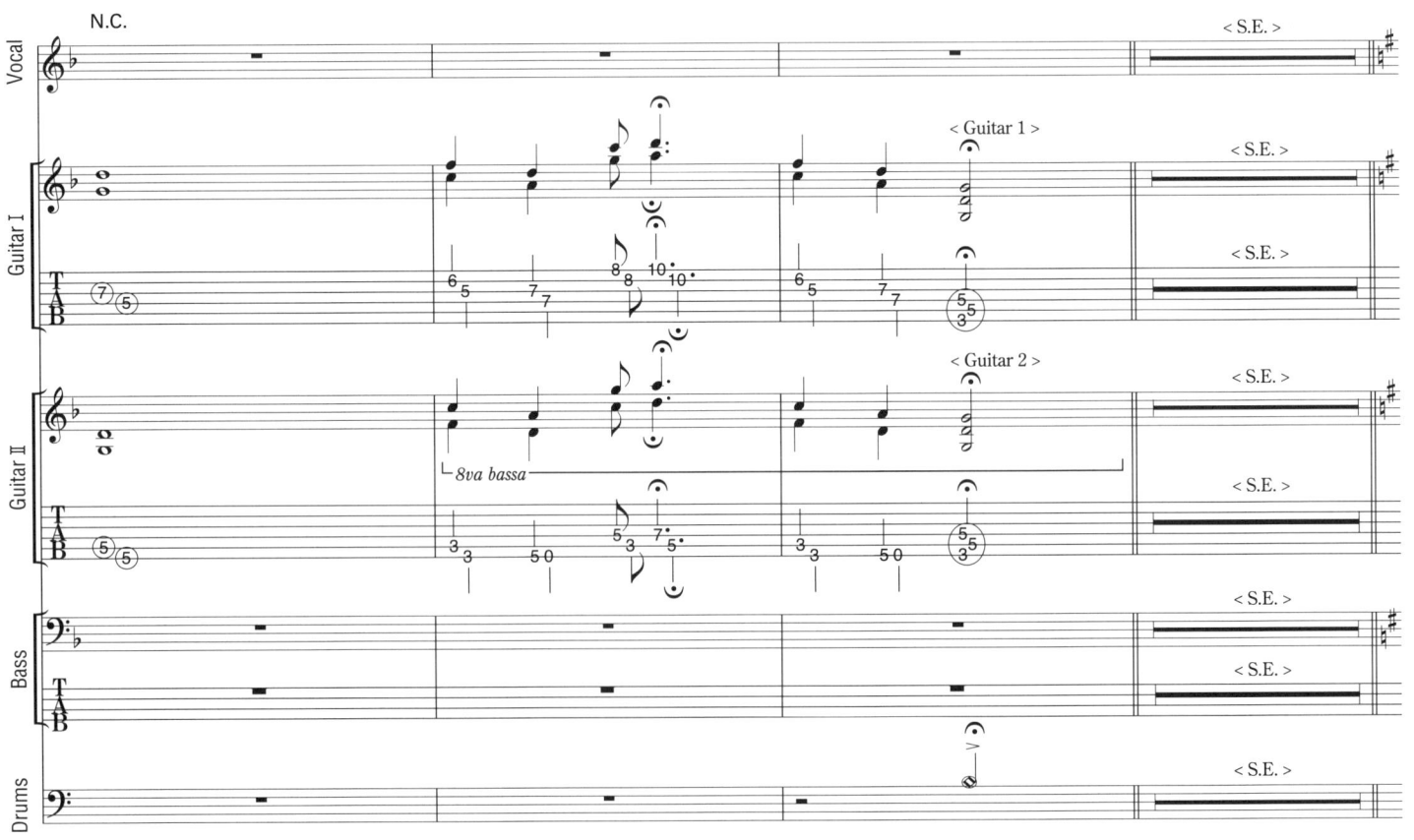

A
A
G D(onF♯) C G(onB) A
Vocal
Guitar I
Guitar II
Bass
Drums
A
G D(onF♯) C G(onB) A
Ooh, yeah, ooh, yeah!

A
G
D(onF♯)
C
G(onB)
B
A
Vocal
Get your par - ty gown an' get your pig - tail down an' get your
Guitar I
Guitar II
Bass
Drums
P
P
A
G
D(onF♯)
C
G(onB)
A
heart beat-in', ba - by.
Got my tim - in' right an' got my act all tight, it's got -

A G D(onF♯) C G(onB) C E
Vocal
- ta be to-night my lit-tle school ba - by. (Your) mom-ma says you don't that your dad - dy says you won't an' I'm boil -
Guitar I
Guitar II
Bass
Drums
E G A
- in' up in - side no way I'm gon-na lose out this time. Oh, no.

196

197

Vocal
Guitar I
Guitar II
Bass
Drums
A G D(onF♯) C G(onB) A
all I ev er get from your, your fam - i - ly ties In tact, I don't think I ev-er heard
A G D(onF♯) C G(onB) G E
a sin-gle lit-tle civ-il word (from) those guys. (But you know) I don't give a light, I'm gonna make out al - right. I've got a

E
G
A
Vocal
sweet-heart hand ___ to put a stop to all that. (Snipin' an' grousin' alright.) Tie ___
Guitar I
Guitar II
Bass
Drums
H
D
A
___ your moth-er down, ___ tie ___ your moth-er down. ___ Take your lit - tle bro-ther swim-min' with a brick, that's al - right. Tie ___

D
G
D(onF♯)
C
G(onB)
Vocal
your moth er down, tie your moth-er down. Or you ain't no friend of
Guitar I
Guitar II
Bass
Drums
A
G
D(onF♯)
C
G(onB)
mine. Ooh, no friend of mine!

201

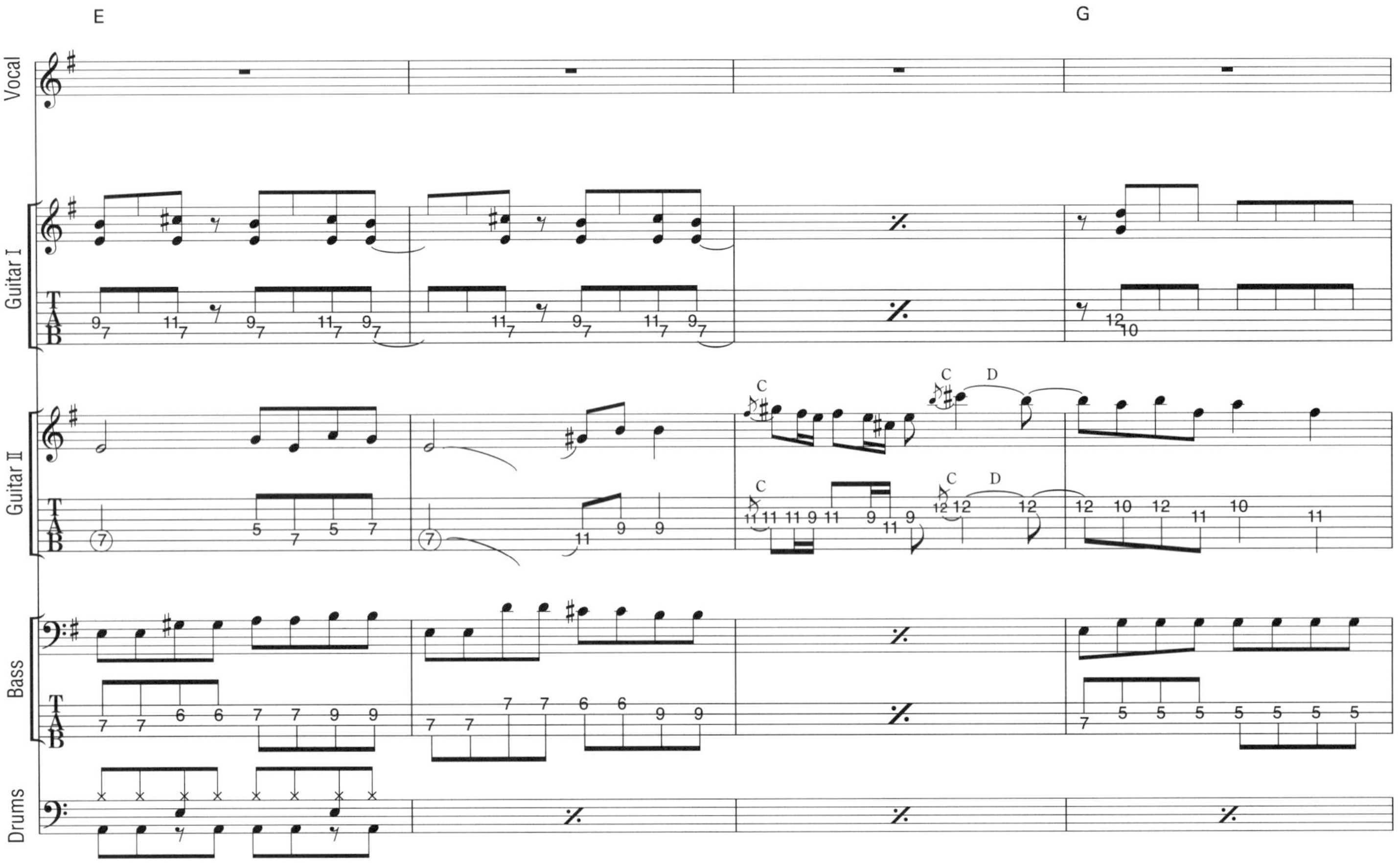
E
G
Vocal
Guitar I
Guitar II
Bass
Drums
C
D

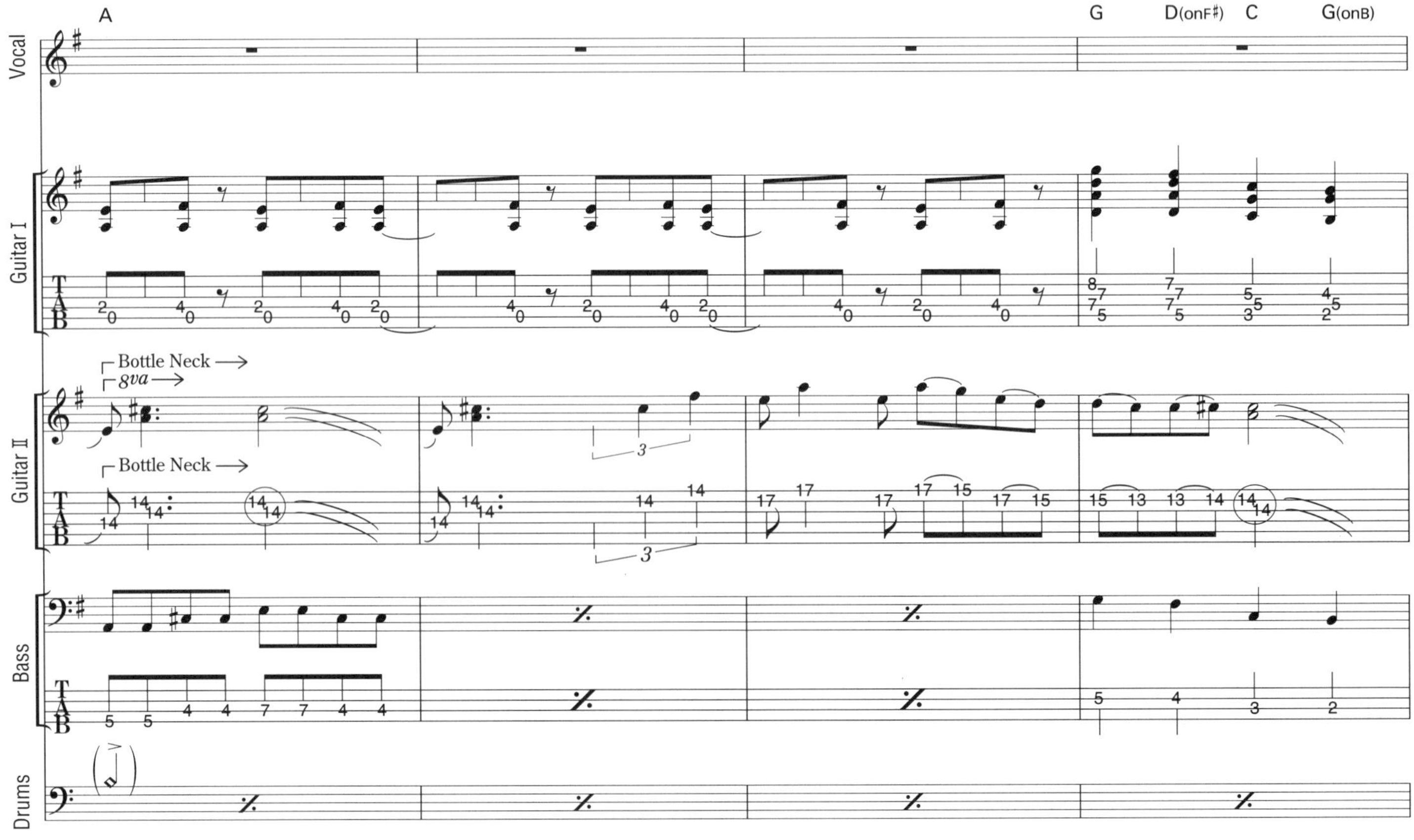
A
G
D(onF♯)
C
G(onB)
Vocal
Guitar I
Bottle Neck
8va
Guitar II
Bass
Drums

A
G D(onF♯) C G(onB)
Vocal
Your
Guitar I
Guitar II
(8va)
Bass
Drums
J
E
G
mum-my an' your dad-dy gon-na plague me 'til I die. They can't un-der-stand it just a peace lov-in' guy.

Vocal
Guitar I
Guitar II
Bass
Drums
A
Ooh.
Oh,
tie
(Bottle Neck)
K
D
your moth-er down,
tie
your moth-er down,
get that
big, big, big, big, big, big
dad - dy out the door.
8va
C
g.

205

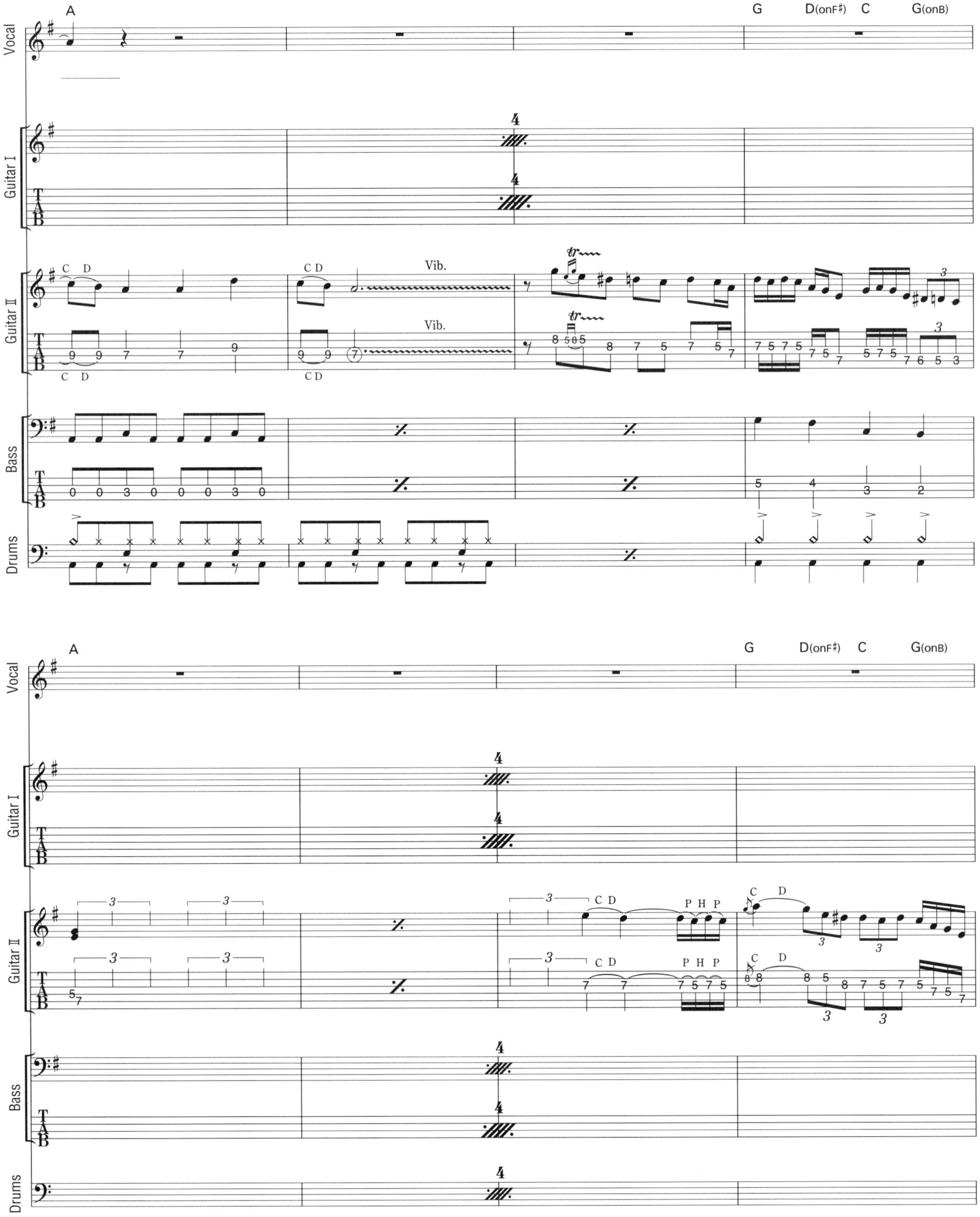

A
G
D(onF♯)
C
G(onB)
Vocal
Guitar I
Guitar II
Bass
Drums
C D
Vib.
P H P

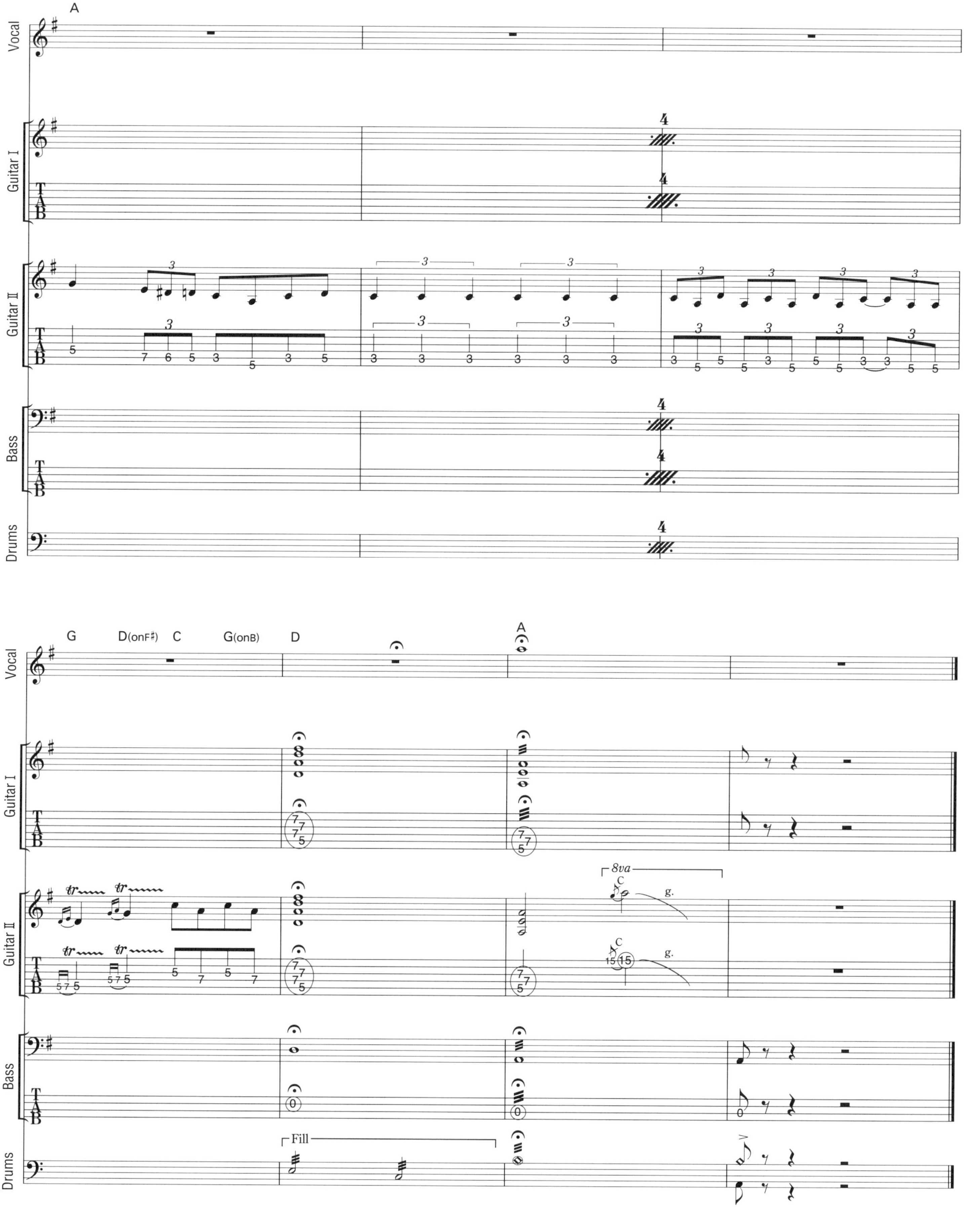
A
Vocal
Guitar I
Guitar II
Bass
Drums
G
D(onF♯)
C
G(onB)
D
A
8va
Fill

We Are the Champions

Words and Music by Freddie Mercury

© 1977 QUEEN MUSIC LTD.
All Rights for the U.S. and Canada Controlled and Administered by BEECHWOOD MUSIC CORP.
All Rights for the world excluding the U.S. and Canada Controlled and Administered by EMI MUSIC PUBLISHING LTD.
All Rights Reserved   International Copyright Secured   Used by Permission

209

I've had my share of sand kicked in my face but I've come through.

And I need to go on and on and on and on.

We are the champions, my

Dm
B♭
C
F
Am
Vocal
friends,
and we'll keep on fight - ing till the
Other
Keyboard
Guitar
g.
Bass
Drums
B♭
F♯dim
D Gm
C(onG)
end.
We are the cham - pions,
We are the cham - pions,

Vocal
Other
Keyboard
Guitar
Bass
Drums
B♭m
B♭dim
F
E♭(onG)
We are the cham - pions. No time for los - ers, 'cause
We are the cham - pions. Ooh, ooh.
A♭
B♭
C7sus4
E
Fm
we are the cham - pions of the world.
we are the cham - pions

I've tak-en my bows, and my curtain calls.

C(11)
Cm
C(11)
Cm
Vocal
You brought me fame and for-tune and ev-'ry-thing that goes with it, I thank you all.
Other
Keyboard
Guitar
Bass
Drums
Cm
G
E♭
E♭7sus4
E♭
But it's been no bed of ros - es, no pleas - ure cruise.
(8va)

I con-sid-er it a chal-lenge be-fore (the) whole hu-man race and I ain't gon-na lose.

And I need to go

on, on, on, on. We are the cham-pions, my

216

217

218

C(onG)
B♭m
B♭dim
F
Vocal
cham - pions, we are the cham - pions. No time for
Other
cham - pions, we are the cham - pions. Ooh,
Keyboard
Guitar
Bass
Drums
E♭(onG)
A♭
B♭
C7sus4
los - ers, 'cause we are the cham - pions.
ooh. we are the cham - pions.

We Will Rock You

Words and Music by Brian May

Bud-dy, you're a boy, make a big noise playing in the street, gon-na be a big man some-day. You got
Bud-dy you're a young man, hard man, shout-ing in the street, gon-na take on the world some-day. You got
Bud-dy you're an old man, poor man, plead-ing with your eyes, gon-na make you some peace some-day. You got

© 1977, 1978 QUEEN MUSIC LTD.
All Rights for the U.S. and Canada Controlled and Administered by BEECHWOOD MUSIC CORP.
All Rights for the world excluding the U.S. and Canada Controlled and Administered by EMI MUSIC PUBLISHING LTD.
All Rights Reserved   International Copyright Secured   Used by Permission

NOTATION LEGEND

The music in this book is transcribed with the utmost attention to detail. However, it is recommended that you listen to the recording and pay close attention to subtle nuances and untranscribable rhythm of the music.

Please note that the music for each part is transcribed in a different format. For instance, for the male vocal, guitar and bass guitar parts, the music is noted an octave higher than the actual sounding pitch. The music for a keyboard instrument such as the piano is noted at actual pitch. Please keep the foregoing in mind when playing the keyboard part using a guitar.

Now we would like to explain the notation in this book for the guitar, the bass guitar and the drum parts respectively.

GUITAR

The following are the explanations for each symbol:

1) C : Bend
- C → Bend (whole step)
- HC → Bend (half step)
- 1HC → Bend (whole and half steps)
- 2C → Bend (two whole steps)
- QC → Slight Bend (microtone)

Letters or numbers printed before the C represent how high a note is to be bent.

2) U : Prebend (string bent before picking)
The U is considered different from C as the string is bent before picking.

3) D : Release
Release the bent string to its normal pitch. This D is equivalent to the latter half of Bend (or Prebend) and Release.

4) H : Hammer-On

5) P : Pull-Off

6) S : Legato Slide

7) tr : Trill (a combination of a fast Hammer-On/Pull-Off)

*Even if any of the above specified notes are combined with slurs, only the first note is to be struck.

8) gliss : Glissando
The Glissando is similar to the Legato Slide (S), however it does not designate exactly where the slide starts or where it ends. Since Glissando occur frequently, in some areas the note "gliss" may be omitted. Instead, slanted lines are used to express ascending and descending.

9) ～ : Vibrato

10) Harm : Natural Harmonic

11) (Ph): Pinch Harmonic
Add the edge of the thumb or the tip of the index finger of the pick hand to the normal pick attack.

12) ↓ : Tapping
Hammer the fret indicated with the pick hand finger.

13) ✗ : There are three meanings to this note.
1. A vague note which its actual pitch cannot be recognized.
2. A note impossible to tell its pitch (rare).
3. Fret-Hand muting with the left hand in a chord form (percussive tone).

BASS GUITAR

The notes are in bass clef (F clef). Some symbols for the bass are similar to those of the guitar, so it would be necessary for you to learn the above-mentioned guitar notations before you play.

DRUMS

From the space above the top line of the stave; G:Tom-tom, E:Snare drum, C:Bass tom-tom, A:Kick drum, ◇ on higher B:cymbal, ✗ on higher B:high hat (o → open, × → close), ✗ on lower F:high-hat (hit by pressing the pedal)

223